Love is spelt T.I.M.E.

Don & Heather Double

New Wine Press

ISBN: 1 874367 57 4

NEW WINE PRESS
P.O. Box 17, Chichester, West Sussex PO20 6YB, England.

Typeset and printed in the UK by Sussex Litho Ltd, Chichester, West Sussex.

Love is spelt T.I.M.E.

Don & Heather Double

New Wine Press

Love is very patient and kind,
Never jealous or envious,
Never boastful or proud,
Never haughty or selfish or rude.
Love does not demand its own way.
It is not irritable or touchy.
It does not hold grudges and
  will hardly even notice when others do it wrong.
It is never glad about injustice,
  but rejoices whenever truth wins out.
If you love someone you will be loyal to him
  no matter what the cost.
You will always believe in him,
Always expect the best of him,
And always stand your ground in defending him.
All the special gifts and powers from God
  will some day come to an end,
But love goes on forever.

(1 Corinthians 13:4-8, Living Bible)

In what is necessary, unity;
In what is dubious, liberty;
In everything, love.

Augustine

Love Is Spelt T.I.M.E.

Time is one of the most valuable things we have, yet it is also something that every person in the world shares equally. No one has more time than anyone else. We all have twenty-four hours in each day. However, although we have the same amount of time, we all use it very differently.

The demands upon our time seem to increase daily; often at the end of a busy day I catch myself wondering "where has the day gone?" When I first started work, people worked much longer hours. At that time, very few homes had the modern conveniences of dishwasher, washing machine, tumble-drier or vacuum cleaner. To own a bicycle meant you were doing well. Today most people take these household tools for granted, and also computers, mobile phones and answer phones. If we are to believe the salespeople, all these household aids are supposed to save us time. Do they? If they do, what are we doing with the time that we have saved?

How do you spend this valuable resource that you have? Do you use time well, or do you find yourself wasting it? I want to address this issue particularly in the area of relationships, and to think about the time we need to invest in our families. Every relationship we have needs maintaining with love. The famous passage from 1 Corinthians 13, printed at the start of this book, is what I will use as the foundation of our thinking.

Think about the relationships you have – in the family, at work, with neighbours, in the church, with peers. For each person in your life, are you using your time properly? Could you express your love to them in a better way? 1 Corinthians 13 is a good place to find the answers.

If you measure yourself against the standard of 1 Corinthians 13:4-8, you are likely to find areas in which you are lacking in love. Being real about our weaknesses is OK, that is how we begin to improve our walk with Father God. However, He is a God of change who gives us every opportunity to move on with Him. Personally, I have changed in many ways over the years and you can too.

In 1994, Heather and I celebrated our Pearl Wedding Anniversary. While I was away on a crusade, I received a very special card from her which read:

> "The card you hold in your hand is a very special card,
> Not just because it is from me,
> But because it says something I want you to know today,
> That I want you to remember forever.
>
> Within the words of this card I want to say
> That you are incredibly special to me.
> You are so important to my days
> And so essential to the smile within me.
> That certain space where our lives overlap
> Is the place that brings me the most understanding,
> The most peace and the nicest memories
> And a joy that comes to my heart so constantly.
>
> When you hold this in your hand,
> I want you to think of me, smiling softly at you
> And thanking you for all that you are to me".

You may feel that this is a very personal thing to share in a book. Well I do too, so I asked Heather's permission to include it. I know that every word of that card is true and I could have sent something similar to her. You see, after thirty years of marriage my love for Heather is as strong now as it has ever been; a key reason is that we have spent lots of time working to improve our relationship.

I am very concerned that today so many Christian families are breaking up. The sad truth is that many people view marriage as something that they can easily end. If you have had a broken marriage, do not be condemned. I too was married before I became a Christian. That marriage broke up, but God gave me a new marriage that He intends to last. Both Heather and I have committed ourselves to each other; we are in this for the "long haul". Family was God's idea, and we can never improve on what God intended; all we can do is follow His plan more carefully.

The best gift parents can give to their children is to love each other and to express that love and devotion every day. Being a parent is not just a title; it is a relationship. A young woman once said, "would someone please tell my father that love is spelt T.I.M.E.?" We live in a world where people are caught up in a "rat-race"; many believers share that frantic lifestyle. Too many young people from Christian families are crying out for their parents to take time with them. They want them to be involved in the things they like doing, to be real with them, to show them true love.

I want to emphasise that building a natural, exciting relationship with your children is a very spiritual thing to do. Husbands and wives, parents and children need to have quality time together; this time will, I believe, help to build up the spiritual strength of everyone in the home.

You must show your family that you love them by your actions and the simplest way to do that is to always keep your promises. The Bible speaks very strongly about this issue. "*It is better not to vow than to make a vow and not fulfil it*" (Ecclesiastes 5:5). To make a promise to your spouse or your child and then fail to keep it will seriously affect your relationship. When breaking promises becomes a regular habit, your family will no longer believe you. People should know that Christians keep their word. When I have promised something to a member of my family and fulfilling it has been tough for me, that is when I have found that love really is spelt T.I.M.E.

Love Suffers Long

Most modern translations start 1 Corinthians 13:4 with "*love is patient*". Patience has everything to do with building genuine and sincere relationships. For Heather and I it has been a constant challenge throughout our marriage. It has not been easy, it took both time and effort, but today we are much more patient with each other!

One day a friend of mine was ministering to people who had responded for prayer. Asking one person what she needed, he got the reply, "I want the Lord to give me more patience." My friend responded by laying his hands upon her and praying, "Lord, please give my sister tribulation!" That horrified the lady and she quickly shouted "No! No! I need more patience – not tribulation." My friend responded by saying that he had only prayed in line with scripture, as "*tribulation worketh patience*" (Romans 5:3, KJV).

When we are serious about building relationships, patience is one of the most important virtues we need to practice. Patience means spending time understanding one another, reconciling things where we disagree. It may even mean we have to accept their point of view and honour them in it. Patience waits for the right time to broach a particular subject. Too often we become so consumed with a particular issue that we do not notice when the other person has their mind on something else. The result is that we fail to properly sort out either issue.

Patience exercises self-control. Many of us have been used to living our own life, doing our own thing in our own time. "I want it, NOW" is a totally selfish attitude; sadly it is one I meet too often when helping a couple to sort out their relationship. The same principle applies within the family. Heather says that a most important time in the growth of one of our children came when she sat patiently for two hours. She was waiting for them to come to the place where they could say "sorry" for something they had done. It was worth the wait, as ever since that day they have apologised easily and promptly. As parents we will often need to manifest the fruit of patience before our children become mature, well-balanced adults.

How does God view patience? "*A man's wisdom gives him patience*" (Proverbs 19:11); "*the end of a matter is better than its beginning, and patience is better than pride*" (Ecclesiastes 7:8); "*being strengthened with all power according to his glorious might so that you may have great endurance and patience*" (Colossians 1:11).

"Long-suffering" is the phrase the King James Version often uses for patience, and it describes God's attitude to us. His long-suffering, especially with the children of Israel, is a model for our relationships. God will never give up on us, so do not give up on your relationships, whatever anyone has done to you.

Having children will develop your perseverance and patience! In the midst of sleepless nights, when baby will not sleep, would you describe your attitude as long-suffering, or frustrated anger? I have noticed that the first year of parenthood usually is a good developer of patience! There is rarely a queue for suffering, but in relationships, especially family relationships, long-suffering cannot be avoided.

Love is patient! Love suffers long! These are inescapable factors in living a real life in the Kingdom of God. If we say we love someone, we have to take time to be patient.

Love Is Kind

"*When the kindness and love of God our Saviour appeared, He saved us, not because of righteous things we had done, but because of His mercy*" (Titus 3:4-5). Expressing kindness is an important way to show love to a person. The word means to be considerate and tender, acting in a thoughtful way and being generous in everything we do. As with patience, kindness is also a fruit of the Holy Spirit (Galatians 5:22).

To be kind can be both aggressive and sensitive. By aggressive I mean that sometimes we will have to take action to stop someone getting hurt – sympathy will not be enough. Equally, being kind means not invading a person's privacy; waiting for the appropriate moment to share something is evidence of kindness. It is kind to help bear one another's burdens and to relieve pressure. Kindness is all about learning to be sensitive to each other.

How else can you show kindness? It could be by doing things that inconvenience you. Perhaps it means doing something you dislike or making an effort when you simply don't feel like it! For me, that has included going to the beach with the family when I would have chosen to be elsewhere. I have made sand castles, played beach games, paddled in the sea, and even gone out in the dinghy although I couldn't swim!

Stephen, one of our sons, came home from Junior school one day saying that another child at the school was regularly picking fights with him for no reason. Normally, he really enjoyed going to school, but he was clearly beginning to develop a bad attitude. We prayed about it with him and sent him off the next morning with a determination that the situation would be different. We also reminded him of Jesus' teaching (see Matthew 5:39) that he should not retaliate but react with kindness and love.

Later that day, when Stephen came home from school, we were eager to know what had happened. He delightedly told us that our prayers had worked and that the boy had in fact been quite friendly towards him all day! Take time to pray with and to teach you children what the Bible tells us about kindness; show them how it should operate in our lives as Christians – it will bear fruit.

Your spouse should be your best friend, and so you should be looking for regular opportunities to express your love to them. God has made us to be creative, so look for new ways to express kindness. Modern living puts great demands upon our time that crowd out opportunities for us to express this creativity. However, don't let that be an excuse for neglect. I have found that as the years press on, the joy Heather and I share makes the effort well worthwhile.

As you probably know, Heather and I spend much of our time travelling the world. We are very used to eating meals in other people's homes, at restaurants and hotels. Often we come across a new food dish that I really enjoy. At that point Heather will make a note and at some future date seek out the recipe and make is especially for me. I know that preparing food is not something that interests her very much, so as an expression of her love to me, these meals are times I appreciate very much.

Kindness will always make time to find ways of expressing itself in giving. On occasions this may mean sacrificing what we want to do to show kindness to our spouse or family. Whatever form it takes, kindness is something which every member of our family, our friends and our work colleagues should come to expect from us. If we want to become more like Jesus, we must show kindness even to our enemies, just as He did.

Love Is Never Jealous Or Envious

Jealousy is usually considered a negative term, but it can be positive when it originates from pure love. The Bible clearly states that God is a jealous God (see Exodus 20:5 and 34:14, Numbers 11:29, Deuteronomy 4:24, 5:9 and 6:15). So we can be righteously jealous too. Let me challenge you to become more jealous of the things of God than you are today.

Paul said, "*I am jealous for you with a godly jealousy*" (2 Corinthians 11:2). He was expressing a specific concern that this church would not stray into deception. Paul would do everything he could to keep them from the enemy. He wanted them to have a relationship with Jesus Christ that would be pure. God wants us to have this kind of jealousy.

Negative jealousy, though, is a very destructive force, quickly destroying relationships. It is so powerful that some versions of the Bible call it a spirit (e.g. Numbers 5:14, KJV). Within families, siblings can often become jealous of each other, especially at birthdays and other times when presents are given. I often meet people who felt that their parents favoured brothers or sisters ahead of them. The result has been bitterness and resentment which damages their life.

In our own family, when our children were small, one of them was very compliant, easy to handle and rarely needed discipline. The one closer to them in age was very strong-willed and constantly needed correction. We had to make sure that we did not favour the one who was easier to handle. We did this by always bearing in mind the danger of crushing the spirit of the one who needed more discipline.

Jealousy, in 1 Corinthians 13, is twinned with envy. We need to note here what James says, "*for where you have envy and selfish ambition, there you find disorder and every evil practice*" (James 3:16). Obviously this sort of envy can spoil any relationship. Do not be envious of what others have, their success, or the recognition and rewards they receive. If you have done something well and nobody else knows, remember that God has seen you. Aim to get heavenly rewards not earthly ones. If you are still reliant upon the praise or thanks of men, ask God to release you; seek to do things only for your unseen Father who does see all that you do.

At Good News Crusade events I often let others, whether guest speakers or team members, speak at prominent times in the programme. I have surprised people when I have been willing to give "the platform" to them; some people have even complained because they wanted to hear me ministering. Nevertheless, this is my heart, and the best way I can describe it is that I am willing to be "the little toenail on the little toe in the body of Christ". I want to simply do the job that God has given me to do, effectively and efficiently. If I do that others will be blessed in an abundant way. You see, love wants the other person to be really blessed; I am glad that allowing others to speak at our events is not an issue for me. To me, it means that God has done a work in me already. Paul says that we must "*be devoted to one another in brotherly love. Honour one another above yourselves*" (Romans 12:10).

Is there an issue that is causing you envy? Take time to consider it from the other person's perspective. So often we do not stop to weigh the matter, but respond immediately based on what we feel. The temptation to be jealous and envious will always be with us. However, when we are obedient to the word of God then we will find victory. James says, "*submit yourselves, then, to God. Resist the devil, and he will flee from you*" (James 4:7). Note that the order is important – most people try to do the exact opposite, resisting the temptation first before submitting to God.

To put aside jealousy and put on respect and honour of others is a tough thing. What priority will you be giving to this battle from now on? Paul says that "*those who live according to the sinful nature have their minds set on what that nature desires; but those who live in accordance with the Spirit have their minds set on what the Spirit desires*" (Romans 8:5). If we allow the Holy Spirit to control us, jealousy and envy will go. Seeking God for His Spirit to be evident in our life in this way will always be costly, because it will demand our time.

Love is never envious or jealous. It is only God's love inside you that will make you always want to give to others. Jesus said "*freely you have received, freely give*" (Matthew 10:8). Have you received from Him today? If not, then ask right now. God wants to fill you with more of His love. This alone will enable you to freely give, so take the time to receive and then to give. When God's love controls you every day, others will see the evidence of that plainly in all your relationships. How well are you doing?

Love Is Never Boastful Or Proud

The Bible says, "*all of you, clothe yourselves with humility toward one another, because, 'God opposes the proud but gives grace to the humble'.*" (1 Peter 5:5). If we become proud, we are in a "no-win" position. God will be opposing us and He will always win. Who wants to have God on the opposing side, anyway?

Humility is a badge clearly worn by those whose hearts are full of love. From my earliest days as a Christian I was taught that the way up is always down. We need to get down at the feet of Jesus, down before His cross. When you get there He will always lift you up. Luke records these words of Jesus, "*When someone invites you to a wedding feast, do not take the place of honour, for a person more distinguished than you may have been invited. If so, the host who invited both of you will come and say to you, 'Give this man your seat'. Then, humiliated, you will have to take the least important place. But when you are invited, take the lowest place, so that when your host comes, he will say to you, 'Friend, move up to a better place'. Then you will be honoured in the presence of all your fellow guests. For everyone who exalts himself will be humbled, and he who humbles himself will be exalted*" (Luke 14:8-11). Expressing love like this is not easy because it is totally contrary to human nature. However, the good news is that the Holy Spirit is inside you for just this purpose. He wants to help and encourage you to become more like Jesus and put on His nature.

It is very sad when a relationship degenerates into a war of words, but this is often what pride will promote. Solomon makes it clear that "*the tongue has the power of life and death*" (Proverbs 18:21) and "*reckless words pierce like a sword*" (Proverbs 12:18). A person who allows pride to rule them will often become both defensive – "how dare they talk to me like that" – and aggressive – "I'll show them." The result will be saying things that are regretted later.

How often have you said, "I wish I'd never said that?" You cannot take back words once you have spoken them, however much you may regret them. The wounds they cause can go very deep often resulting in long-term damage, especially to loved ones. It is never too late to allow forgiveness to cleanse you, but it is obviously much better to walk humbly and hold your peace.

I often stay in other people's homes and something I always take note of is the godly quality of the children. I have met several with the outstanding manners, humble spirit and servant's heart that God wants. On one occasion one boy made a special impression on me. He was eleven years old and appeared to be a "model" child. I know his father quite well and I can see that what is in him, he has reproduced in his son. One thing that stands out is that the father has been more concerned with attitudes than actions; I believe this was the key to his success. Getting the correct attitude into your child will produce the right actions. I believe this lad has a tremendous future ahead of him in the Kingdom of God. My prayer is that those of you reading this will want the same for your children.

If you are aware that you have failed in this area of pride don't delay putting things right. One way in which you can begin to restore things is to humble yourself by apologising and asking for forgiveness. Doing it will be tough; you must be real and be specific in your confession, not just saying a general "I'm sorry." This will really help your child to see that things have changed, and recognise that you love and care for them as a genuine person. It is then that they will know that love is spelt T.I.M.E.

Love Is Never Haughty, Selfish Or Rude

The dictionary definition for haughty is – "arrogant, cavalier, contemptuous, disdainful, scornful, supercilious." Quite a list to measure ourselves by, especially if we think we might be like it! It is interesting that the Bible talks in the same terms, "*A proud and haughty man, 'scoffer' is his name: he acts with arrogant pride*" (Proverbs 21:24, NKJV).

Some people find it very easy to act in a haughty way towards their partner and others. I believe this can occur, for example, when one partner is better educated than the other. I had tuberculosis when I was a boy and missed most of my schooling. When I left school, I could not even write my own name and address. When I met Heather, I was still very poor at reading and especially at spelling. Heather, on the other hand, had received a Grammar School education and had spent some time in Further Education. She could easily have dominated me and made me feel inferior. However, this did not happen because Heather believes, as I do, that when two people are married they become one (see Ephesians 5:31). Both people bring their natural and spiritual gifts into the marriage. Together, by complementing each other, they have everything they need to equip a wonderful partnership.

As a warning, please note another verse from Solomon, "*Pride goes before destruction, a haughty spirit before a fall*" (Proverbs 16:18). The reality is that someone with a haughty spirit will fall in the end. Someone who persists with this attitude **will** fall! If you think this may be you, bring your attitudes to the foot of the cross now and determine to change.

Something that makes me really sad is the number of times I see how easily people are rude to each other. We can define rudeness in many ways – being discourteous, impertinent, impolite, abrupt, curt, tactless, and crude. What a dreadful list! Yet I often see all those attitudes in the church as much as they are in the world! Even to ignore each other is rude. Next to God, my wife is the most important person in the universe to me. I would be embarrassed to ignore the Lord, so I ought to be embarrassed to ignore my wife too. The same principle also applies to our family. I heard a man explain how he corrects his children when they are discourteous or impolite to their mother. He tells them, "You are being rude to my wife and I will not allow that!" This father has instilled in his children the reality of the relationship he and his wife enjoy; he has also taught them to respect that relationship.

Rudeness can also express itself in immodesty, indecency and coarse jesting. That of course includes your family's attitude to sex. What are you teaching them? It should be an open subject within the family, never talked about in a dirty way, but treated as something pure and beautiful. Your priority should be to teach your children, preferably before they reach puberty, that sex is God-created. He made sexual love wholesome, clean and to be entered into only within a marriage relationship. By example, teach your children to avoid unclean talk, smutty jokes and the world's attitude to sex.

Within the security and protection of your family you need to warn your children about things like pornography. Sadly it plagues our society, being so freely available in newsagents and book stores. Do you realise that your child will be exposed to pornography at school and in your own home? Do you control what they watch on the TV? You must teach your children to recognise the dangers and how to avoid them, even when their friends are involved.

My parents strongly built into me "manners maketh man". I believe it is still a gracious thing when a man gives preference to a woman, even today. For a husband to open the car door for his wife or to help her put on her coat, does express love. Young people showing respect for the elderly should not be regarded as outdated. The Bible teaches us to "*rise in the presence of the aged, show respect for the elderly and revere your God*" (Leviticus 19:32). Isn't it interesting that respect and reverence for God are linked in this passage? Teaching these things to your sons and daughters is a wholesome contribution to family life.

Spend time with your family teaching the virtues I have mentioned; some may call them old-fashioned. However I strongly believe that you are showing genuine love to your children by sending them into the world with these solid foundations. The world is full of rudeness, haughtiness and lack of respect, but your children do not have to conform to this pattern. Train them to be generous, respectful, and well-mannered – good ambassadors for Christ.

Love is spelt T.I.M.E.

Love Does Not Demand Its Own Way

Every man and woman alive has to fight to control selfish attitudes. All of us continually face this battle. Selfishness is a common trait, but we need to recognise it for what it is – SIN. We can only deal with it at the cross of Christ. We must dethrone selfishness in our lives and replace it with servanthood. How do you identify this attitude? Simply, if you find yourself saying "What can I get out of this situation?" that is selfishness. It is summed up in two words "I want". The opposite is servanthood, which asks, "What can I contribute? What can I do? Can I help?"

Often, I am invited to speak at Men's Meetings, and my favourite topic is to teach about developing unselfish attitudes. I believe that it is a foundational virtue for every man As my friend Edwin Louis Cole says "Christlikeness and manhood are synonymous." Jesus set every man the high standard of complete selflessness. Often ladies contact me after such an event to ask, "What did you do to my man? He came home so different!" The letters and conversations I have, testify that these men no longer demand their own way; Jesus has made them more considerate and caring. Most often, wives comment that their husbands are developing the attitudes of a servant. That is very special, watching as the Holy Spirit transforms a man.

Selfishness in a marriage is often evident in the area of sexual relationships. One important key to overcoming it is to give each other time. We should never rush sex; to create a romantic feeling in your spouse will often take all day, not ten minutes! I believe that every time you have sex, your overwhelming motivation should be to fulfil your partner. If that is not your attitude, ask the Lord to change you. He wants to restore your intimacy with your spouse, but be aware that intimacy costs – it takes time.

I have discovered over years of counselling that a frequent cause of problems in this area is late night TV. If either partner watches TV late into the night, it can seriously affect their relationship. It may seem trivial but it does rob them of having enough time alone loving each other. It will also be a likely cause of tiredness, which experts have long recognised as a factor in spoiling a couple's sexual relationship.

Selfishness can also be a problem with our children. A parent/teenager relationship is unique; it will only ever be successful when you, the parents, take time to develop it. "Rules without relationship equals rebellion" is more than a glib statement. If your child is rebelling, look closely at your relationship with them. It may help to ask a close friend, who knows you both, for advice or direction. If you feel that your relationship could be better, make the effort to give your child time. Rules about what they can and cannot do, may need relaxing if they are getting in the way of your relationship. The important thing is to make the environment as helpful as possible to build up the relationship. What a delight it was, both to Heather and myself, when our children, as teenagers, maintained a close relationship with us. Giving them time was costly but the results are immeasurable.

Wanting the best for another person and not seeking selfish gain is the true way of love. "*For where you have envy and selfish ambition, there you find disorder and every evil practice*" (James 3:16). The scriptural contrast to selfish ambition is for you to "*be devoted to one another in brotherly love. Honour one another above yourselves*" (Romans 12:10). The world teaches that thinking only of yourself is OK, particularly if you want to be a success. The way of Christ has no room for that attitude.

The Bible clearly teaches us to put others before ourselves. This is the only way to love our wives and families. Spend time building up the other members of the household instead of pushing yourself forward.

Love Is Not Irritable Or Touchy

When we allow ourselves to become irritated, we manifest a lack of love just as much as if we had wronged someone physically. Although we like to treat some sins more seriously than others, murder above unbelief for example, the Bible clearly states that there is no distinction. Irritability is a manifestation of anger; it is something our Heavenly Father wants to remove from our lives, as He transforms us into the likeness of His Son.

The best way to deal with irritability is not to grit your teeth and hope that next time it won't happen. What you should do is ask the Lord to fill you with His caring love, which alone can defuse tense situations. However, this change does demand that you settle in your mind that you will not respond in this way again. Though you will face the temptation to repeat that old habit, hold firm and positively take the opportunity to express love. "*God has poured out his love into our hearts by the Holy Spirit*" (Romans 5:5), so draw on that to enable you to stand firm.

One area where men need to be especially sensitive is when our wife, daughter or other ladies we spend time with, have their monthly periods. We need to be aware of the hormonal changes that occur and make allowances for their behaviour, if they are "under the weather". Teaching your sons how to properly respond to their mothers and sisters at this time is important; this principle is one Heather and I used with our sons. When one of them was engaged, his fiancée came to Heather and said, "Thank you so much for teaching your son how to respond to me when I have my monthly period. He nearly always backs off from any potential confrontation at this time, understanding how I am feeling."

People often express irritability by being "moody". A moody person is someone who often has sudden changes in their temperament. They have peaks and troughs: one moment they seem happy with life, the next they are finding fault with everything and everyone. This type of person, in my experience, also becomes easily depressed. We should not accept this as normal for Christians; Jesus came to set the captives free. If you are someone who struggles with mood swings and depression there is hope for you. Come to the foot of the cross and let God's love flow and heal your spirit and mind.

Being oversensitive can be an expression of irritability. I am sure you know people who overreact in situations: either moodily, by drawing into themselves, or in anger, with a sudden outburst of words and actions. People who withdraw and sulk, especially in public are not honouring God or themselves. Others "go over the top" with extreme emotional outbursts. Some become uncontrollably hysterical, some violent, others become hyperactive, the common factor being actions that demand attention. They do not enjoy the peace of God in their lives and are unable to rest in His goodness. I don't think that a follower of Jesus should accept this as normal, do you? James says that "*man's anger does not bring about the righteous life that God desires*" (James 1:20).

When you get angry, how do you react? The way you handle your feelings will determine whether you sin in your anger. God, I believe, wants us to be able to express anger, in a righteous way, about the things that anger Him. Proverbs 6:16-19, for example, talks of things God hates and we should hate them too. Our aim should be to allow the Holy Spirit to show us what He is angry about, so that we can mirror His feeling to the world.

We can always control anger successfully by growing the fruit of the Spirit of self-control, for "*against this there is no law*" (Galatians 5:23). If you need to change in this area ask Jesus to pour more love into your heart right now; it will take time, but look for the fruit of self-control in your life. You, and those around you, **will** see both your attitude and speech change, praise God. Taking the time to "grow" self-control will show others that you care for them.

Love Does Not Hold Grudges

Love, Paul says, "*will hardly even notice when others do it wrong*" (1 Corinthians 13:5, Living Bible); he also tells us to "*get rid of all bitterness*" (Ephesians 4:31). The writer to the Hebrews instructs us to "*see to it that ... no bitter root grows up to cause trouble and defile many*" (Hebrews 12:15). If you hold on to a grudge, or remain bitter towards someone, it will eventually turn into resentment. That is often the start of physical sickness. It is said of Esau, after he had sold his birthright, that he realised how foolish he had been. However, "*when he wanted to inherit this blessing, he was rejected. He could bring about no change of mind, though he sought the blessing with tears*" (Hebrews 12:17). Holding a grudge can lead you to a place where it holds you and will not let go.

Grudges are very harmful to relationships. A "chip on your shoulder" will hurt your spouse, children and others you are close to. People who hold grudges often continue with a relationship but constantly snipe and criticise, inflicting wounds which hurt very deeply. As I have said throughout the book, there is only one answer to this, love. Love will bring feelings of bitterness into the open without condemnation and heal the pain.

Heather and I have met people who have held grudges against someone in their family and have not spoken to them for days, weeks and even years. Once I met someone who held a grudge against a child they were responsible for and did not speak to the child for three weeks! They served meals and did all the usual things one has to do when looking after a child, but that was all. Later in life the child needed ministry for the damage this caused.

Love will hardly even notice when others do it wrong! Other translations say that love ...

> "*keeps no record of wrongs*" (NIV);
> "*does not keep account of evil*" (JB Phillips);
> "*doesn't keep a score of the sins of others*" (The Message);
> "*doesn't store up grievances*" (New Jerusalem Bible)

When Heather and I conduct marriage seminars, we often emphasise that this is an important principle for staying happily married. Many spouses hold on to memories of events, especially of little things, in which they think they have been wronged. True love says that when a wrong has been done you will hardly notice that it happened.

Do you realise that when you ask your Heavenly Father to forgive you, He completely erases the wrong, as if you had never sinned? Too often, when Christians have been unable to forgive themselves of the guilt of sin, they go back to God and say "Forgive me, Lord." He says, "What for? I can't remember that sin!" The point I want to make, is that when He completely erases forgiven sin from our account, God chooses not to recall what we have done. His Word says that He is "*faithful and just to forgive us,*" so believe it! He does not forget what we have done, He chooses not to remember! So must we.

It is sad, but there is so much confusion about this subject, which for me is so clear. Jesus said, "*whenever you stand praying, if you have anything against anyone, forgive him, that your Father in heaven may also forgive you your trespasses. But if you do not forgive, neither will your Father in heaven forgive your trespasses*" (Mark 11:25-26, NKJV). Note, Jesus used the word "anything". Do you believe it? It is the truth! It has nothing to do with who is right or who is wrong. Apportioning blame is not the issue. Put simply, we **must** forgive, otherwise God will not forgive us.

I believe that a problem often occurs when people try to forget but they don't forgive. That is not right. If you harbour an issue in your heart, you have not truly forgiven. By an act of will you must reject the memory **and** confess aloud that you have forgiven the person who upset you. "I forgive you!" are important words of release. For me, forgiveness is the greatest love word in the world. Jesus set us a wonderful example as He hung on the cross and said, "Father, forgive them." Let me encourage you to do as He did and forgive, unconditionally.

If you struggle with that idea, you must recognise that God says "Do it," so do it! Remember, even if you find it really hard to forgive someone, by being obedient to His word, you release His grace into the situation. Do not forget that His grace was sufficient for you and me when we were unbelievers and on our way to hell. His grace is sufficient to allow His love to flow into the deepest areas of resentment and unforgiveness in our lives. Take the time to forgive!

Love Is Never Glad About Injustice

"*Love is never glad about injustice, but rejoices whenever truth wins out*" (1 Corinthians 13:6, Living Bible). What a challenging word **never** is. I wonder how many of us could pass the test if Jesus measured us against this standard? Nevertheless, despite failing sometimes, I trust that it is a goal that you are always aiming for. Love needs to be the focus of every motive, attitude, action and reaction.

The Bible has a lot to say about injustice. For instance, "*Better a little with righteousness than much gain with injustice*" (Proverbs 16:8). "*He has showed you, O man, what is good. And what does the Lord require of you? To act justly and to love mercy and to walk humbly with your God*" (Micah 6:8). God is just, He hates injustice. Micah makes it clear that those who love the Lord will know what He requires of us. When God requires something of us, it is wise to take note and act upon it.

So, we are to "*rejoice whenever truth wins out,*" or as the NIV puts it, "*delight in the truth.*" If we are to delight and rejoice in the truth, it is important to understand what Paul meant. Joy and delight are not just feelings but are responses as well. Do you react joyfully when you are treated kindly, or when you see an act of love? You can choose to be joyful.

To delight in the truth will demand total honesty; it means nothing should be hidden and we must bring everything into the light. The apostle John wrote, "*if we walk in the light, as he is in the light, we have fellowship with one another*" (1 John 1:7). This verse mentions two key words concerning our relationships. The word "walk" is referring to our conduct, the way in which we behave. The word "fellowship" expresses something about how we relate to others. God commands that we walk "in the light" in every relationship we have: in our family, in church, in business, with neighbours and anyone else we meet. In all things and with everyone we know, we must walk in the truth.

During a Good News Crusade Married Couples Weekend, we ask that the couples write a letter to each other. In this letter they must write about seven specific areas of their marriage. One point is to tell their spouse something they have never told them before. It is amazing how significant that part of the letter can be, and how the Lord uses that revelation. Sometimes it has been a devastating secret that they have shared. However, in the end sharing that truth has saved the marriage from being torn apart.

We live in a time when many leaders in our society set an unholy example. Today, it is hard to find a totally honest man who has a central role in government, industry or another position of authority. Being "economical with the truth" is a phrase which sadly now describes common business practice. The truth is not the truth unless it is the whole truth, for there is no elastic in the truth!

One dictionary definition of injustice reads: prejudice, discrimination, inequality, partiality, favouritism. We should eradicate all these from the church. Paul wrote that "*if one part suffers, every part suffers with it; if one part is honoured, every part rejoices with it*" (1 Corinthians 12:26). Too often the truth is that in the church "when one person suffers we all rejoice and when one person is honoured we all get jealous!"

The only way we can effect a change, is to ask God to pour out His love upon every person in the Church. We must pray that His love will pervade every part of every relationship. God is all seeing and all knowing, both of our thoughts and our actions. Use this knowledge as a motivation to promote truth, honesty and justice. Jesus set us the example by always being just; it is attainable if we spend time in His love.

Love Will Be Loyal

Love is loyal no matter what the cost. The first loyalty in any family should be between husband and wife. Marriage is a lifelong commitment demanding constant loyalty from both partners.

Loyalty to our children is also very important. Christian parents often find it hard to be loyal to their children if they have turned away from God; responding properly to a child who is rejecting your faith can be very difficult. Yet staying loyal to them is probably the best way to get them back. To do so will take effort. As I have already suggested, an excellent way to express love is to show a real interest in the things they are interested in. You can win them back to Christ by simply being a good friend, rather than reminding them of their shortcomings.

When our son Stephen was almost 16, he decided to taste a little of the world and he backslid. I was naturally concerned and spent time praying about what I should do. One day I felt God give me a clear instruction: "Give all your time to Stephen whenever you are at home." Heather accepted what I heard was from God and was in total agreement; so, whenever I was at home I made myself available to Stephen. I took him out for meals; I got involved with his sports activities; I listened to the music he enjoyed and taught him to drive.

When we were shut in the car together alone, we related as Dad and son better than we had ever done before. Looking back, I think this period was one of the best times of my life as a father. His backsliding ended about seven months later. By giving myself to him he learnt a lot about his dad. I showed him that I love him, had time for him and would not let the devil have him.

Disloyalty is most often expressed in the things that we say. Saying negative things about our spouse or our children can have tragic results. Heather and I are often shocked at the way people talk disloyally about their spouses. Sometimes wives start to tell me things about their husbands, or husbands about their wives, which I consider to be totally disloyal. You may dislike things in your partner's life, but to gossip about them to others is the worst thing you can do. If you feel that your spouse is flawed the best way to encourage change is simple. Get a piece of paper, list their good points and commit yourself to only encourage your partner. It is surprising how soon people change and grow in the warm glow of encouragement. Cold, hard criticism always has the opposite effect.

Many scriptures teach us about the fruit of what we say. Let us consider a few: "*The tongue that brings healing is a tree of life, but a deceitful tongue crushes the spirit*" (Proverbs 15:4). "*Pleasant words are a honeycomb, sweet to the soul and healing to the bones*" (Proverbs 16:24). "*No man can tame the tongue. It is a restless evil, full of deadly poison. With the tongue we praise our Lord and father, and with it we curse men, who have been made in God's likeness. Out of the same mouth come praise and cursing. My brothers, this should not be*" (James 3:8-9). These scriptures are self-explanatory and need no amplification. We need to be **real** about letting the Word of God shine its light into the dark places of our mind and heart. How do you measure up to these verses? If you need to change, let the Holy Spirit do His work in your life.

After you have spoken hurtful words, saying that you did not mean them is pointless – the damage is done. You can repent, let the blood of Jesus cleanse you, and even ask the person to forgive you for what you said. Nevertheless, **you can never, ever, recall the words you have spoken**. Those words that cause pain can never be withdrawn. If speaking without thinking, or saying hurtful things is a problem to you, it is time to change. The most important step in changing a habit is the decision to change. It may also help to tell a friend what you have done so that you make yourself accountable to change.

One way to nurture a relationship is to make the person you love feel secure. As with all of the points in this book, you need to invest time, as feeling secure means learning to trust. If your loved ones know that you are always "covering their back," they will have confidence in you. We all need to know that our friends are protecting and standing up for us. "*Hatred stirs up dissension, but love covers over all wrongs*" (Proverbs 10:12). Love is loyal, so take time to be loyal.

Love Will Always Believe

To always believe the best of someone is a very healthy and positive thing. It shows that you have faith and trust in them.

Think for a moment about a road bridge. As you approach the bridge, you will often see a sign which tells you the maximum load the bridge can take: five, ten, twenty tons, or perhaps more. The sign says that the bridge can safely carry this weight; any more will put it under such stress that there is the possibility of it collapsing. The same principle works in our relationships. The strength of the bridge of trust determines what can be spoken, seen, heard, written and even thought between the two partners. To build a strong bridge will take a great deal of time, but that bridge of trust between you is crucial. If that trust breaks down, the relationship will struggle to survive. If you cannot trust someone, you will be suspicious of their motives and actions and this can have catastrophic results. Measuring the strength of your "trust bridges" will reveal how strong your relationships really are.

As I shared with you earlier in the book, my first marriage ended in divorce. When Heather and I were married, on one occasion I said "I will never trust another woman again!" I spoke out of the hurt and rejection I still carried from my divorce. That one statement seriously affected my relationship with Heather for some time. After we had resolved this situation, Heather told me that she often had to try hard not to let me down. If she said she would do something, she made sure she did it, so she would not add to my distrust. Today, we have built a strong bridge of trust; we know that no matter what we discover about each other, the bridge is strong enough to survive. It has taken hard work, but it has been time well spent, and it has produced a high-quality relationship.

Some people find it hard to understand that God expects us to believe in people. They think that we should only really believe in God. The Bible gives us several good examples of people who believed in others. Jesus even said that if we cannot believe in others, especially God's people, then we are going to find it hard to believe in God. "*If you believed in Moses, you would believe me, for he wrote about me, But since you do not believe what he wrote, how are you going to believe what I say?*" (John 5:46-47).

Jesus' own brothers did not believe in Him, despite knowing the circumstances of His birth. "*For even his own brothers did not believe in him*" (John 7:5). Our society is one that holds up cynicism and scepticism as virtues. It is sad but trust and belief, values that God says are pure, are now seen as naive and almost worthless.

Sometimes we have to break through the "pain barrier" when confronting issues. Yet our love will deepen as we remain totally open and honest with each other. Our love will grow as we determine to make the time to get closer to each other. As time goes by, our love will deepen and grow; the fruit is that we will increasingly trust and believe in each other.

Finally, do not forget that Jesus believes in you even if you have trouble doing so. He has a plan for your life which only you can fulfil. If you have children, He has given them to the best parent they could possibly have! He believes in you so much that He died for you. Believe in your family, your wife and children, believe in your God, believe in yourself.

Love Will Expect The Best

What do you expect from a relationship? Your answer will depend on why you established it in the first place. However, we need to be realistic about our expectations. Too often a friendship, even a marriage, will break down because one partner's expectations are beyond the other's ability to achieve.

For a relationship to be meaningful I believe that we can expect each other to give our very best. However, when someone fails, even repeatedly, we must not forget that they are human and we need to be big enough to forgive. If a relationship does get into difficulties, that is when you will both see the value that you place upon it. It will determine how much time you are willing to give to work a problem out. I love Paul's exhortation "*finally, brothers, whatever is true, whatever is noble, whatever is right, whatever is pure, whatever is lovely, whatever is admirable, if anything is excellent or praiseworthy, think about such things*" (Philippians 4:8). Think about your family, friends and the people you meet each day. If they are not Christians, even if they are, do they let you down? (It is worth saying that many of us have high expectations of our fellow Christians, but we forget that they can still fail). Let me encourage you to take this verse from Paul's letter to heart. If people have let you down, start to look for the things that you can admire, and praise. It may be hard to begin with, but it will quickly produce a strong friendship.

"Shalom" is a Hebrew word that conveys a greeting. According to the translators, "Shalom" expresses the wish of the one who says it, that the hearer should receive every conceivable blessing that God can give. When a Jew uses this word, they are saying more than hello, they are expressing generosity and expectancy. Try expressing that to a few friends and see what a difference it makes!

Expecting the best will deal a death blow to the nit-picking attitudes that often develop between many husbands and wives. If we love our partner in a way that always believes the best, we will look only for the best. It is amazing how much good you can discover about your spouse that will cause minor irritations to disappear.

Many parents expect their children to be the best behaved in the neighbourhood, school and church; sometimes, I believe that they are in danger of being unrealistic. Too many people believe that their "little Johnny" could not possibly do anything wrong. Love must always be realistic. It will help us to discipline them in the way that will produce the best in them. "*The Lord disciplines those he loves, as a father the son he delights in*" (Proverbs 3:12).

I have met parents who think that when their child has a period of disobedient behaviour, even backsliding, that means it is all over; they have lost them and failed as parents. Do you remember the story about my son earlier in this book? He got into some serious situations during his period of backsliding, but came through it and God is using him today in amazing ways. Do not think your child has ruined their future or that you have failed as a parent during one of these crises. There is always hope in Jesus.

What do you expect from your child? What do you pray for them? The best answer is that you want them to reach their full potential and discover the place in life that God has planned for them. However, Christian parents sometimes try to make their children into prayer warriors and students of the Word by the time they are eight or nine! They forget the needs children have to kick a ball, dig sand castles, play with imaginary friends and climb trees. Here is a warning. You can produce a rebellious child by making them grow up too quickly, or to be too "spiritual". Having Jesus' love in your heart will help you to give space and time for your children to enjoy the fun of childhood.

"*Our hope for you is firm, because we know that just as you share in our sufferings, so also you share in our comfort*" (2 Corinthians 1:7). Hope is a strong, positive, biblical word. There will be times in every relationship when the other person is going through a tough time. Whether it is our spouse, one of the family, a business associate or friends in the church, Paul says we should share in their suffering.

Relationships are about "give and take," so what are you giving? Do you build confidence in the people around you? Are you encouraging them to hope? Is it the best or the worst that you expect from friends? If someone you love is suffering, they need you to respond willingly and positively. People who really love express it by putting in time. If you set your heart to consistently do that, others will know you as a good friend.

Love Will Always Defend

Genuine love is the strongest defence of all. To defend someone means we will "cover their back," be loyal and protect them. Who would you instinctively defend, no matter what the cost? List the people you would do that for; now, think about the people God says you should love. Which list is longer? Would you be prepared to defend everyone on the second list? Jesus said, "*love your enemies and pray for those who persecute you*" (Matthew 5:44).

If someone makes an accusation against a friend of yours, how do you react? The righteous way to defend them is not to start arguing, but to put Matthew 18:15 into action. Ask the person if they have spoken to the one they are accusing themselves. If they have not, then they have no right to be talking to you about the issue. Insist that they do so immediately. If they refuse, you must challenge them about why they feel the need to make such accusations.

I have had this experience several times recently concerning the move of God which many parts of the church have been experiencing since 1994. People have been making accusations about several men God has been publicly using. They have warned me to keep clear of these men because they are supposedly in error. Each time an accusation has been made, my response has been simple. I have asked "Have you heard this man speak? If you have, did you take the opportunity to express your concerns to him directly?" Sadly, the answer has been "No" every time. Whatever the issues involved in this current blessing, we make the choice to stay righteous. If you have a concern, do something about it, but do not accuse, condemn, or gossip. It is my experience that most of the men involved publicly in what God is doing are extremely gracious, humble men. Without exception they are willing to talk, to stay sensitive to God's voice and to learn.

Very often an accusation of this nature begins when someone says, "I am sharing this 'in love'." That phrase always makes me cautious. I have learnt that it usually means that the person is trying to justify something they should not be saying. Gossip is a horrible thing and can cause great damage in the church. Satan uses it often to attack those in leadership. Someone told a good friend of mine, via some gossip, that I had been divorced and had remarried. He refused to believe it, until much later when he found out that it was the truth. The point I want to make is that his love for me made him reject the piece of gossip he had heard. Without this love, he could easily have believed a rumour which would have seriously affected our relationship. Love ensured that we are still friends.

"*Though one may be overpowered, two can defend themselves. A cord of three strands is not quickly broken*" (Ecclesiastes 4:12). This scripture is one I often use to teach husbands and wives to bring God into their marriage. However, I want to comment on the statement "*two can defend themselves*". The unity of a husband's and wife's relationship will produce a strength that becomes a shield of defence against attacks and accusations. One of Satan's main strategies is to destroy marriages and family life, particularly Christian ones. His attacks are often vicious, for he is a killer (John 10:10). A husband and wife are a team; I believe that they need to spend time doing things that will build a strong and healthy partnership between them. This will involve making time for each other and looking for those areas of weakness where disunity could grow. By working on the weak areas, by being committed to defending each other, couples will quickly build a strong defensive relationship, an impregnable fortress.

Husbands and wives need to be united in the way they raise their children. They must have the same goals. If parents are not united, concerning discipline, for instance, it will cause confusion in their children. If a mother habitually says to her children "wait until your father comes home," and does not discipline them herself, what does that produce? The children will not only think that Mum and Dad have different values, but they may even develop a fear of their father's return.

Heather and I were raised in excellent families, but both had different emphases. When we began to raise our own children, we found we both needed to adjust. For twenty years, our parents worked a deeply engrained set of principles into our lives while we lived at home. When we came together to train our children, we discovered differences in our approaches. However, we worked hard at producing a united method which eventually produced good fruit.

Unity then is a godly means of defence. It will keep a marriage strong and a family content, well balanced and together. As with everything else in this book, love is the key. When we let Jesus motivate our actions and thoughts, we will defend our friends and relatives. The love of Jesus will be the motivation that ensures our families are as secure as they can be.

Love Will Create A Home

Home! What is a home? Home is where love is! Home is where I like to be, where I am accepted, where I can put my feet up, relax and know that I am loved! A house can be full of the best furniture in well designed rooms, equipped with every imaginable convenience, but it remains a house until love moves in. Home is a place where you will find discipline, security and peace. It can be materially poor – as many homes I have visited around the world are – but the essential ingredient is love. Home is a place where we forge strong relationships and where love finds its fullest expression on this earth.

Jesus said, "*those whom I love I rebuke and discipline*" (Revelations 3:19). So, discipline is an essential part of love and is one evidence of true love in a family. Pure love will not forget to discipline. Allowing our children to love without discipline is leaving them to fend for themselves. It is contrary to the word of God, (read Proverbs for some good examples). A family needs clear boundaries, which, when clearly laid down, bring effective security to the home. I will never forget the Christmas Day when one of our sons misbehaved and I took him into another room and spanked him hard. A few days later he came to me and said, "I want to thank you Dad for spanking me, I needed it." He was fifteen years old and it was the last time I ever had to spank him. He knew I loved him.

To cultivate the best relationships in your home will require time

- to develop and discover all the qualities which each member of the family has to contribute
- to make the family the fullest expression of love that God intended it to be
- to build something that will last for as long as you are upon this earth.

Relationships within the family will change as the years go by, because children grow up; however, in all the changing patterns of your family, the relationships which are forged during those early formative years will continue.

Modern society, with all the various demands upon life, is not the best environment for a family to spend time together. Accordingly, we must try to do everything in our power to make sure that the family does spend quality time together. I would suggest that you should try to have at least one meal together every day. I know from experience that this can be difficult with extra activities, particularly after school, but I believe that making the necessary adjustment is worthwhile.

You may feel overwhelmed by the demands on your time I have talked about in this book. You may feel that it is time that you don't have. Before you dismiss the whole principle, let me add that the **quality** of the time you invest is far more important than how much quantity of time you have. Quality time is both focused and relevant to the one receiving your love.

In giving time in the way I have been suggesting, do not look for what you will get from the relationship. Look for the things that will strengthen it and deepen it. To find quality time does not need you to find a lot of time, but it does need to be a regular commitment; also, remember what I have said about keeping your word, in the chapter "Love is Loyal".

Take care to avoid the temptation of becoming possessive; that has destroyed many relationships. We must be selfless and constantly concerned about the other's interests. "What can I do that will bless them?" "What can we do together that will be helpful?" "What can we do together that will give them pleasure?"

The most important point about quality time is the attitude of the people involved. Do you want to be a blessing, to be selfless, to give and build up the other people in your life? If so, even a short time spent together will produce results. I am often asked the question "what sort of thing should we do together?"; so in ending this book I'd like to mention three things that have been a great source of fun and togetherness for our family.

From our earliest years as parents, one of the joys of our family life has been "family nights". Once a month, we set apart a special evening just for the family. The key point was that we spent time together and we allowed no one else to disturb us. (Our house has always been busy, with lots of visitors, so our children needed to know that there was a time when they had our complete attention.) Every member of the family made a contribution – one chose the menu for the meal, another chose a game to play. As it has been a regular event, everyone has taken a turn in choosing each part of the evening. The memories I have of these evenings are very special. However, what I want to express is this: these evenings have been important for us to have fun together, share our friendship with Jesus, and to bless each other.

Family holidays are also times when we have had great fun together; I would recommend them to anybody, despite the hard work they often entail. Some of the most precious memories I have, have been the times when we all went away together. Throughout our marriage Heather and I have also found it important to get away together by ourselves. The principle of special times of rest, relaxation and joy go right back to the beginning. God set us the perfect example (Genesis 2:1-2) and I believe we all need to take the same kind of special time to rest.

I am sure you have heard the statement "The family that prays together, stays together". Every family, I believe, needs regular time together to share devotionally, to enjoy together the relationship you have with Jesus. The format should be one that accommodates every member of the family so they can be involved. "Devotions" should express a real love for God, and love and care for each other.

With our children, we started when they were very young, so that now they can never remember a time when they did not take part. I am convinced that this was a crucial part of the development of their own spiritual lives. For many people I know the "Family Altar", or whatever it is called, is a time that is boring and lifeless, to be avoided at all costs. For me, family devotions have always been great fun, something to be looked forward to and never missed. The reason for the difference has been that we have always tried to focus them on our amazing friend Jesus.

Everything that I have spoken about in this book comes back to the same point. Our marriages, families and every other relationship we have, need regular oiling by genuine godly love. Without this love, everything we do will be as nothing to the Lord. The tough part of 1 Corinthians 13 says that if I don't have this love in me and working out through me, "*I am only a resounding gong or a clanging cymbal,*" "*I have nothing,*" and "*I gain nothing.*" I have always felt these verses are among the most sobering in the whole of the Bible. Working out all that is in 1 Corinthians 13, so that it becomes a reality in your life will inevitably produce great demands on your time. Nevertheless, remember that the more love you get from Jesus, the more you can give. Love **is** spelt T.I.M.E.

Appendix

Do you Love God?

"*All the special gifts and powers from God will one day come to an end but love goes on forever*" (1 Corinthians 13:8, Living Bible). Love goes on forever because God is love and God is eternal. The most important relationship a person can have is with God. To quote a friend of mine, "the real secret of life is learning to live life in relationship with God." That is not a cliché but a reality.

A relationship with God is always one filled with love. "*We love because he first loved us*" (John 4:19). If you want to know what love is, take a long look at what Jesus did at the cross. Perhaps the best known verse in the Bible is John 3:16: "*For God so loved the world that he gave his one and only Son, that whoever believes in him shall not perish but have eternal life*". To give His only son meant that God gave all He had. What amazing love! Consider the cross and realise the rejection, suffering and agony which Jesus went through. He did it just for you and me. Jesus took the punishment that you and I deserved for every sin we will ever commit. It is incredible, but Jesus loves us that much. How can anyone refuse such love?

If we take time to think about Jesus' crucifixion, the love He displayed there must surely bring us to repentance. We have to realise what our sin did to Him. Each of us must acknowledge our responsibility for His death. Then as we begin to allow the love of God to change us, something will happen. We are born again into a new life with Christ. This is the beginning of the most important relationship we will ever have. God is our Father, Jesus is our Saviour and Lord and the Holy Spirit is with us, enabling us to live in His presence.

If you have never had a relationship with God in a personal way, you can, now. Use this prayer as a guide:

> **Lord Jesus Christ, thank You for Your love for me. I need to receive this love into my life today. Thank You for dying upon the**

cross in my place. I now repent of my sinfulness, and accept your sacrifice for the forgiveness of my sins.

Come into my life to be my Lord and Saviour. Please lead and teach me for the rest of my days. Come, rule and reign in my life and teach me your lifestyle of love. Thank You Lord. Amen!

If you have prayed this prayer please write to me (or send a fax) at the address at the end of this chapter. I would like to send you a free study that will be of further help to you.

Imagine for a moment a newly-wed couple. They enjoyed a beautiful wedding service; yet, they were so nervous when they exchanged their vows that neither of them felt that anything had really happened. Concentrating hard on saying the right words meant that they missed the enormous change that had taken place. The truth is that from the moment that they spoke their vows, their lives were utterly different.

In the same way, when you prayed this prayer you entered a new relationship with the Lord Jesus Christ. From that instant He has become totally committed to you, for life, even if you do not feel very different. The most important thing in your life now is spending time with Him. The time you spend with God will develop and deepen your relationship with Him.

Loving God can never be a halfhearted experience. For it to work effectively we have to give it all we have got. A religious man once asked Jesus which is the greatest commandment. He replied, "*Love the Lord your God with all your heart and with all your soul and with all your strength and with all your mind.*" (Luke 10:27). "The Message" is a new translation of the New Testament by Eugene Peterson. In it this verse reads "*Love the Lord your God with all your passion and prayer and muscle and intelligence*". If we really do this, no part of our lives will be left unaffected.

Yet God does not stop there, He asks more of us than just to love Himself. "*If anyone says, 'I love God', yet hates his brother, he is a liar. For anyone who does not love his brother, whom he has seen, cannot love God, whom he has not seen*" (1 John 4:20). Our love for God and for each other should be so intermingled that the two cannot be separated! We cannot love God and ignore those around us. Every day, we must express real, godly love to everyone we meet. This is the way we will show how much we love God.

You may contact Don Double at the following address.

GOOD NEWS CRUSADE
17, High Cross Street
St. Austell
Cornwall
PL25 4AN

Other publications available from **GOOD NEWS CRUSADE**

The Three Dimensional Woman

Rediscovering Devotion, Character & Victory

by HEATHER DOUBLE

Heather wrote this book because she became frustrated that the majority of books written for Christian women left her feeling that unless she was a wife, mother, or had some special problem, there was nothing God had to say to her. It comes from Heather's desire to write and help women, of all ages and cultural backgrounds, to enter into a deeper relationship with God for themselves.

For the best results...

Follow the Maker's Instructions

How to Have the Best in Your Marriage and Family Life

by DON & HEATHER DOUBLE

Follow the Maker's Instructions is a thoroughly biblical book. It states boldly and uncompromisingly that marriage and family life are God's idea and it still works at the end of the 20th century. In clear terms, Don & Heather set out the "Maker's Instructions" and show how they can be practically applied to every marriage and family.

Available from your local Christian Bookshop, or from:

Good News Crusade,
17 High Cross Street, St Austell, Cornwall PL25 4AN